The Now

June Hall, who now lives in Bath with her husband and two
teenagers, began her career in the editorial department at Faber
& Faber where she trained and eventually became established as
an editor. She then moved to paperback publishing and
afterwards went on to set up a successful literary agency.
When – quite unexpectedly – Parkinson's Disease was
diagnosed in 1996, she began to write herself and started
publishing in various poetry magazines.
This is her first collection.

Praise for *The Now of Snow*:

'June Hall's work records, with wit and without sentiment, the relentless encroachment of a debilitating disease on a *normal* life, that is, one in which fulfilment and frustration form two sides of the domestic coin. Neither the disease nor the domesticity are allowed to dominate: there is no demonising or sentiment here, just the all-too-human effort to value life as it passes and to understand how we are changed against our will. There is an honest depiction of our frailties, both social and physical.

Poetic form and trenchant humour are wheeled into service as a bulwark, as in the villanelle *Fine*. She shows that parody, in the right hands, is not merely a satiric device, but another form to be redirected. As she says in a poem on Klee, art depicts what makes us individual by becoming individual in itself: *it disobeys, laughs, splits in two*. These poems are full of that disobedient, very human energy.'
W.N.HERBERT

'June Hall's poetry evokes memories and emotions which move the reader. She startles and satisfies with unexpected phrases which are so apposite to the poem. A welcome new voice to look out for in the future.'
PATRICIA OXLEY, *Acumen*

'I'm delighted to support and endorse this very readable and moving book of poems from someone who has Parkinson's Disease but is not dominated by it. I'm particularly delighted that 50p for every copy sold will go PD research which is in such urgent need of funding at present.'
MARY G BAKER, MBE, *President, European Parkinson's Disease Association*

The Now
of Snow

JUNE HALL

BELGRAVE
PRESS·BATH
BELGRAVE PRESS • BATH   7 BELGRAVE ROAD, BATH BA1 6LU

First published 2004 by
Belgrave Press, Bath
7 Belgrave Road,
Bath,
BA1 6LU

(No submissions please.)

ISBN   0-9546215-0-6

Cover design and typesetting by
Paul Mitchell Design Ltd. 01628 664011

Printed in Great Britain by
The Cromwell Press, Trowbridge, Wilts.

for my family
and in memory of Pip

Acknowledgements

Thanks to the editors of the following magazines in which some of these poems have appeared: *Acumen, Equinox, First Time, Iota, Poetry Nottingham International, Orbis, Poetry Scotland, Seam, Staple.*

Many thanks also to Julia Green, Greg Hall and my Wednesday writing group as well as other writing friends for their endless patience and support; to Patricia Oxley of Acumen for her early confidence in me; to U.A.Fanthorpe and Rosie Bailey for their generous gift of time, encouragement and gentle toughness; to the poets and tutors at Arvon and elsewhere who have taught me so much, especially Selima Hill and Bill Herbert; to Paul Mitchell, a superb designer and Terry Melia and Billy Adair – the best of publishers.

Contents

Our true home is the present moment.
To live in the present moment is a miracle.
The miracle is not to walk on water.
The miracle is to walk on the green Earth
in the present moment...

Thich Nhat Hanh

I

Snakes

I'm here to listen, he says
and smoothes the space between us.
Unlistening he runs
his polished measure over me,
pumps arms, pivots hands,
rotates wrists, commands eye swivels,
beams at the snake spirals he has me draw.
Better than mine, he lies.

Content, he offers me his arm,
and offers too his malediction:
Things will get worse!
Cleanly he chops through hope
then slivers and slices it dead,
conveys with oiled assurance
how others have imagined improvement
only to be proved wrong
for like a slow-moving escalator
the disease, relentless,
will progress.

I query his catechism of certainty.
His suit grows darker, his smile
wider as it cracks around the mouth.

The Shake

Not even
    a spilt cup of tea.
        Everyone's hand shakes
    sometimes,
doesn't it?
    Mine used to
        before.

    Is it better?
you ask,
    Is it worse?
        sneaking a look.
Not much
    on view.

        Getting good at deception.

Right hand
    protects the other,
holds, enfolds,
      substitutes, hides
        – above all –
    hides
like a mother
  who covers for a
    wayward child
  yearns to restore
the peace
    yet fails.

      Left hand
    restrained
      at night
   in the intruder's grip
      shudders,
    wild to regain

        the norm of day.

Stranger

Uninvited, you greet me
circling the web of hands
in the still spaces of the dance
to claim me as your partner.

Your touch startles,
trembles and feathers my hand
like a wounded sparrow
palmed in an unfamiliar hold.

The music trips and sways.
A new tempo
          binds us.

We Two

Prankish like Puck, invisible,
it flutters the print I'm reading,
jitters me with nerve-piercing noise,
shivers my flesh with ice chills.

It intrudes in love-making like
the South Wind at play in the sun
and, when I'm driving, in sterner mood
takes the wheel, arm heavy on mine.

Down the long blind alley of night
it lurks to ambush sleep,
jumps me, half-Nelsons my arm,
squeezes and clamps my leg taut.

Sometimes though it tires, pleads
for me to soften, smile within its grip,
stroke the arm it teases,
hold the hand it's colonized until

I can imagine folding to my care
this other who is now – my self.

Normal

How do you have it – just normal?
Conviction bubbles with the water
as he slides an egg into the pan.
Anthony Sinclair-Jones,
tartan-slippered, silver-haired,
with a wife-shaped space about him,
filters his B&B guests with care.

Middle runny, hard outside, I guess –
like me. Or would it be more normal
for the shell to crack, white wobble and
puddle on the French-tiled floor,
yoke splat on the Aga streaked with blood?

Not breakfast-time British, that,
yet can we really be sure
when we're all in the same pan together
that boiling is normal at all
or that it's so odd to be scrambled?

Fine

I know you want to hear I'm fine
so what the fuck am I to say
when I – of course – don't want to whine?

I don't mislead you by design.
It's true I'm terse. Don't go away!
I know you want to hear I'm fine.

In verse – or worse – I can refine
just how it feels. It's shit – OK?
But I – of course – don't want to whine.

I fumble typing out each line,
my frozen finger trails on a...
and still you want to hear I'm fine.

Pain steals the night. My hand's not mine.
The leg that drags is made of clay.
Yet I – of course – don't want to whine.

My body shakes, it's in decline,
mouth drools, arm cramps, nerves knot and fray.
I know you want to hear I'm fine...
Well, bugger off! I want to whine.

On/Off

Miracle of the day slot on News South West:
successful implant grins *breakthrough surgeon*
as he films the before and after of 'Man with PD'.

What I see is a prisoner in solitary, his face
frozen to a blank. Speech dribbles from lost mouth,
foot stutters and taps a hard-to-crack code
on his hard cell floor. Hand scrabbles and claws.

Couldn't feed himself or shave, we're told,
couldn't swim or laugh or even speak properly!
Now the implant's turned on. He is still. He smiles.

But this is television. The surgeon showman
flicks the switch again, resetting him in helpless motion
to show the power of new technology.
Switched on he's a man. He is still. He smiles.

Switched off he's a broken clockwork doll.

Note: PD is short for Parkinson's Disease

The Truth Trail

She tells us not to fuss –
why's she fussing then?
It's only an old shake.
Adults are so sad!

What should I tell him?
The truth is like a tight-tied sack
whose canvas frays around the seams
and leaks a trail of tell-tale dust.
His finger hesitates to trace
black question marks in what is spilt.

It's nothing, is it?
Though I've heard her on the phone
talking like it was.
What is it she won't tell?

Shouldering alone
the unknown contents of the sack,
I fear its weight would flatten him.
And so I measure out the truth
in tiny less alarming heaps.
He piles them up but doesn't speak.

Untimely

A rope tightens rough around my chest
as I breathe in my bare-topped children,
brush their summer skin, smell their smallness.

Willow arms trail sleep across the bed,
fingers floating towards his teddy. Beside him
his twiggy sister sprawls, drooped on an edge.

These long-limbed saplings need me
firm-rooted and, as in this vigil, still – not
quivering, shaken with disease, old too soon.

The time is out of synch like a match
that burns too fast, searing fingers
when the flame goes out, candles not yet lit.

Stile

It leans the wrong way, tipped into the hill,
grey oak, worn, mis-angled for climbing –
or for rest. Rooted in soil slip it's out of true
like me. I scramble up, shaky from the climb,

perch off-centre on its disobliging frame
and through a tunnel of hips and hazels
watch the valley roll into shadow,
a reminder of the downhill trek ahead.

Gone are my hurtling days
of whoop and bound through thistle fields.
Side steps slide and fumble, nervous of mud
squelched deep by cattle hooves.

The last stile to the road is new,
solid, clean-grained, glowing amber,
paired with a shiny aluminium gate
whose easy swing, unlatched, surprises me.

Funny Devices

You bet! I could be a midlife dare-devil, do wheelies
with my electric shop-rider, carousels on revolving car seats,
swing from ceiling hoists, sponsor power-chair races.

I'd flick easy-to-open bottle-tops at my open-mouthed children,
seduce my man on satin sheets in shiny pyjamas
designed to help the helpless turn in their adjustable beds;

or I'd whiz up and down on my stair-lift, glowing with giggles,
get drunk in the day from a no-spill mug so full of sherry
that no one would know what sort of tremor I'd got.

Not me. I'll junk this mag with its glossy, know-all face
and pasty backside plastered with aids-for-the-infirm,
heavyweight ads that pack a mean punch.

Not me. I'll shred its pages for paper chase trails,
light bonfires with its two-timing cover, bake potatoes
in its ashes. You won't find me on the ropes for long,

a user of funny devices. Not me. Not yet

*Note: the mag is **The Parkinson** published by the*
Parkinson's Disease Society

II

The Now of Snow

An early snowplough's cleared the mountain road,
heaped crystals on either side,
banks that fall into deep-sleeping whiteness.

Puppy-children tumble out, pant heat into crisp air,
yelp and snowstorm one another, belly-flop in
sharp-edged drifts high and soft enough to bury them.

Whooping, they scoop powder-balls, brickbats
to launch against the car while we, caged in warmth,
gaze through a screen exploding with snow,

foresee hands, iced red, too numb to warm,
sodden trouser legs that cling to frozen skin,
feet stuck in shoes heavy with slush, the crying

and the long journey home. Worry shadows the sun.
Somewhere we've grown old.
We nag and fret over wet socks and the lack of boots.

What, for God's sake, is a wet sock
to the dazzle of the moment, the now of snow?

Death by Children

I was dying before
but didn't know it
any more than the midge knows
when she feeds her body to her young.

I flop and sag,
stiffen and cramp,
ragged with a labour
never suspected
when they put you to my breast.

My body's been cut,
stitched and scarred,
pumped, milked,
barred from sleep,
kicked and sicked over,

crazed by crying,
pierced by howls,
weighed down with
carrying and harrying,
kissed and missed
and – many times – re-created by joy.

I learnt I was dying
with the first birth,
tried to guard my space
as though you –
down-wrapped,
crown smelling of
coconut and warm hay –

had no need to feed on my future.

Three Solos

Responding to Mr Eliot

One: Morning
(i)
Plans past and plans future
both perhaps sour plans present.
What might have been and what has been
lead to one conclusion –
a mother's place is in the wrong.

(ii)
Round the still point of the manic morning
whirls the early Monday chaos –
homework, sick notes, hockey sticks,
racquets, morning snacks, back-packs –
swirled from hall to fridge to bedroom,
the hunt for cartons of juice and lost trainers.
Distracted from reaction by reaction,
inoperancy of co-operation,
desecration of the inner sanctum,
the wail of disconsolate children.

(iii)
That was a way of putting it – not very child-friendly.
At this point there is only the clock
– which says eight. *Go, go, go!* say the kids.
Their voices in the back
scrabble, squeal, disagree. We're late
moving yet hardly moving in half-filled jeeps
that block the slow flow over the bridge.
See the faces brushed by terror,
see the road rage simmering –
not here, not the silence of deep sleep,
not the dead hush of the empty house.

(iv)
I drop them on a double yellow
breathing relief into cold air.
To arrive is to undo all our worrying,
and know we've made it for another day.

(v)
The pram is in the hall.
The fog is in the fir tree.
A gym-slip sleeps on the briar rose.

Sibling jeers and slaps echo in the mind
down the hours of sleep never taken,
the plans never realised.

Two: Afternoon
(i)
In my morning is my afternoon,
in my afternoon my morning.
What might have been – meditation,
sun-tanning, novels, working late –
and what has been
remain a perpetual possibility in a child-free world.

(ii)
So here I am in the middle of my life,
entre les années de liberté,
having largely wasted the magic of motherhood
measuring out my life with school runs.
Missed dates and unfulfilled goals
point to one cause
which is always overload.

(iii)
In my pink-paint-peeling kitchen
I had not thought so much undone.
Ketchup-smeared plates, discarded crusts,
half-drunk bottles, blobs of jam,

crumbs and whirled bits of paper
smear and trash the space.
Plans before and plans after.

Clucking from one appointment to the next
mother love cannot bear too much triviality.

(iv)
A time for the afternoon pick-up,
a time for tea and a time for television,
a time for homework and a time for play.
Quick, now, here, now, Mummy, say the kids
demanding complete absorption.
Quick! Quick! Quick!
Hungry children cannot wait,
not now with the wink of the microwave
and the flat face of the wide screen blinking.

The clash of voices and slamming doors
all lead to one end
which is usually crossness.
Muddy feet tramping,
up and down, in and out,
mirth of youth, before the crease of wrinkles
and the slow slide into stodge.

Three: Evening
(i)
After the tear-swept bedtime
when the bath-water's chilled and
the last battles waged and truces struck
will small fingers encircle my neck,
clutch and cling?

Will these children
drift into angel sleep?
Makura Om. Peace upon the pillow.

(ii)

I shall not cease from exploration –
byeways and back roads, rat runs and cut-throughs –
and the end of all my commuting
will be to arrive where I started –
home – and see it for the first time.

(iii)

Here, now, in the failing light
destiny is homebound and child-centred,
destiny is drawn in peanut butter.
When tiredness and headaches are one
and the roar of lost tempers fades
I slump upon the bed,
a condition of complete depletion
not uncommon in parents.

(iv)

But all will be fine
and all sorts of things will be fine
when clouds pass and reflections in the pool deepen,
young faces smile like sunflowers turned to me
or wild roses opening under the apple tree,
when the house is filled with laughter,
the sound of mine infolded with theirs
and the joy and the journey are one.

Softening

You're not so crisp now, Mum!
She measures and nails the year's stress,
fixing guilt precisely with sharp pins.

Yet it's not what she'd call an 'insultation'.
I have been lousy to live with.

Impish, she binds me with tight hugs
but her smiles, unchanged, release me.

First Place

For Katherine

How clear you are you'll win this race!
Your legs grow longer in their stride
since most of all you want first place.

You're out ahead, you set the pace.
Come on! I yell. I'm at your side.
How clear you are you'll win this race!

Two laps are run and near to base
your stamina is fully tried
since most of all you want first place.

Oh help! Someone is giving chase.
Your sense of shock is hard to hide
and yet you're clear you'll win this race.

Tough luck for you, she's on the case.
She's pulling up – will you collide
since most of all you want first place?

Sheer will is written on your face.
You zoom ahead. I whoop with pride
since most of all you want first place
and clearly now – you've won this race!

Essentially

For Richard

Injustice is in the air.
I'm not self-scented! he protests,
sensing a smell that mothers hate.
Am I? The boy voice dips,
shoulders droop, eyes slide away from mine.

Charmed by the new-born word,
bear-hugging, I breathe
the fresh surprise of his cheek,
burrow in the wild flop
of unwashed hair, musty with natural oils,

determined to bottle up
the ten-year perfume of his being
and keep it to remind me always
who essentially he is.

Mezzanine

Hello, downstairs people! he bellows,
Turn off my light! The order drops
through the hollow space between.

He sleeps in the half-timbered mezzanine,
an airless lair which holds the heat of day and
fevered tantrums of his twelve-year growing.

A red *No Entry!* sign, part unpinned,
glares from his door. He yells unaware.
'Between two chairs', the French would say

but when the music stops is it a game
for a little fellow, wet face ready for prayers,
in a rumpled nest, milk teeth under the pillow,

or Russian roulette with grown up weapons
where you grapple and dare, soft soap and swear
and people really get hurt?

No kissing! their stringy man-child roars
so they learn downstairs to unkiss him,
twist into awkward hugs, hold in their love.

But at night he peeps through the wooden rails
like the toddler of his play-pen years and checks
they haven't gone away, his ground-floor people.

Her Father's Daughter

They must be a mistake, breasts
that bud under fresh white T shirt
(strappy version just acquired).

His body is changing too. Homeside man
spills into midlife, belly puddling, while she

throws off the tomboy years, bounces into
flares, blue nail polish, crop-tops, mascara.

Gold arms ring his bear girth. Sleepy,
she pillows her newly pierced ear
on the safe slope of his tummy.

Not on Display

She views us through fashion shades,
two penguins plumped on the pool side,
mangy zoo birds cloaked in striped towels
instructed to tuck in frayed or floppy bits,
cover bodies that, displayed,
will floor her just as once
her sticky tantrums flattened us.

Is it his puffed belly and silver face fuzz
or my brown-spotted, high-veined hands,
puckered thighs, post-Caesarean overhang
that crease her so? Eleven years old,
mounting the narrow catwalk of puberty,
she'd like to cut the flab, model us in styles
worthy to view through fashion shades.

Stillbirth

for Pip

Breath held.

Loop-wire tightened at the solar plexus,
a screen that stares and doesn't move,
the awkward flutter of a surgeon's hand,
keening from a place below the earth.

The baby's dead, he said.

Dark rivulets of hair, a stroking softness,
skin of gossamer too frail to hold,
breasts weeping milk that won't be drunk,
a conch empty of all but echo.

The baby's dead, he said.

That waking pause and sudden knowing,
Baby clothes on rails that must be passed;
the date that cannot be avoided,
words that turn and wear the mind away.

Breath

Both Times

years apart, he hurdled his despair,
that of death, and bent to kiss them –

gossamer son, blanketed in blue,
a tiny flower of blood dried at his nose

and marble mother, shrunk tight
in a coffin ruffled with cheap blue satin.

Like end-stops, one held hope stillborn,
the other cradled ancient disappointment.

He kissed away his shrunken dreams
both times.

Anniversary

November reaches bare-boned to the sky,
branches splayed like starving arms,
a withered straggle of leaves
flagged against the morning mist.

Month of mud and worn-out grass,
stone-cold waiting and silent poppies,
Day of the Dead. A crimson teardrop
hangs from the nose of the stillborn son

I stroke but never hold, scared
his paper skin will flake, twig limbs
melt like snow – summer's growth
all broken up. The years flow back to

that November when, unsuspecting,
my stripped-down heart, bared
to the bleak helplessness of love,
riots with unseasonal blossom.

III

North-South Moon

For my father*

I leave in spring, find you in autumn.
Your sliver moon reclines arched on his back;
mine sits forward smiling at her dreams.
Our skies tilt, distant truths conversely angled.

Crossing the equator, I unravel the nostalgia
embroidered in my summery English name –
sweet pea, lavender, frilly pinks and floribundas
frocked in white.   June doesn't fit.

I was always a winter baby. Cried a lot,
under-fed, struggling to survive an African June
and the upside-down house of my fate
while you looked the other way.

Back to back in the antipodes
common ground bears our weight – just –
and, shifting to a new configuration,
differences rub shyly together.

*Note: *who left England first for South Africa, where I
was born, and then Australia where we met for
the first time in fifty years*

Home

Shipped from India, a displaced child
tossed like cargo from shore to shore,
you were badly damaged in transit.
Aunt Georgie, foursquare like her house,
gave you a home in redbrick Northants,
helped you reconstruct, grow tall.

War picked you up at nineteen,
swung you into action. For a while the Navy
was a sort of home where you played
like a toy sailor, shiny-buttoned,
peak-capped, stripes on your sleeves.

Your peacetime home keeled and crumbled
when death demolished Georgie.
Duty denied leave or compassion.
The trophies of your fragile boy-world –
cricket bats, rugger shirts, photos – all
stripped and dumped by paid executors.

Nothing could be salvaged. War dropped
you, homeless, on the bomb site of daily life.

Note: based on my father's account

Disturbing the Spring

Our ways of care are different.
Mine is an autumn energy, unseasonal
and out of sorts – chopping, digging, scrubbing out
those nameless weeds that smother growth.

In the shy time of the year
bulbs, long hidden, raise tentative shoots.
My sharp-pronged fork probes, not meaning
to snap frail stems or pierce their rising sap. Still
some might-have-been colours, purples, golds
and silky whites, return to earth unopened.

The week brings kinder weather.
I settle the troubled earth – as you would –
replanting, tamping, raking with soft fingers.
Will clearing air the soil
free roots deep, white as anger?

Long-distance Friend

Are you in your tub...? you ask
and sometimes end with *Love*.
An evening ritual, Mondays,
calling London to Avon,

Avon to London.
We talk across the miles
till the bath water spoils,
our voices echoing off

blue tiles and bare boards
connected only by a wire.
We meet – and miss – in the gaps
between sound waves.

Somewhere along the line
feelings, disembodied, knot,
twist like the coils
in my over-stretched phone cord.

Winter hardens.
Other baths fill and empty,
waves slop on the floor,
the temperature drops.

That you're relieved at last
pours down the silence
like cold water unplugged
when I agree to disconnect – for good.

Love soaks away.
I cradle the phone, watch
the final swirl of friendship
sucked into waste.

IV

Distant Summer

(1)

Letters are my fix,
e mails a shot in the arm.
Being remembered

gives me a high. Doesn't last.
Empty box. White screen. I'm down.

(2)

She can delete friends,
scorn e mails that hide unread,
lock the letter-box.

The key to abandonment
hangs on the hook. Leave it there.

At the Beach Café

our waitress is pencil thin,
her smile to the point.

She's twisted a scarf
bright with diamond pattern,
tied it as a gypsy top.

The knot flirts as she twirls
between tables – waiting

Afternoon in Provence

While women talk of this and that
and fan themselves with magazines
his shoulders groan, twist away
from village gossip, bargain prices,
summer recipes and broken nights.

Summer has demoted him,
stripped him down to sandals.
Wary that either sun or women
will flush or peel him over tea,
he shifts apart and stirs his ice,
le maître – teacher without a class.

Haikus

Sandal
opens the foot to summer
like a door to freedom,
toes dusted white in long light.

> **Cloisters**
> White light decorates
> stone slabs worn by countless feet,
> caught through time's arches.

Cornish Sky-line
Herring-boned slate walls
held up with hanging rock. Plants
bind man's plans to God's.

> **Dandelion Clock**
> Glides of soft seed pass.
> Time hangs on the wind. Puff again.
> Unblown hours resist.

> **Over Mist**
> robin flutter-jumps,
> rises, falls on the bright barbs,
> a wink to autumn.

Monday
Crows pegged on high lines
score the sky with music,
call the washday song.

Now
two monks on the road
corner the bend before me,
brown-gowned and smiling.

V

Swept Away

He cuts the summer from her hair,
razors it to stubbled hay.
The flowing sun lies darkened
in the bottom of the bin,
curls that played and swam and
never worried how they looked
are rounded up and swept away,
a discipline of health and hygiene,
locks from each head making way.

He cuts a firm new shape
short and sensible for winter –
not what she wants. Outside
oaks streaked with gold
are losing leaves, their falling
swept into municipal piles
curled,
withered,
carted off.

Must Rush!

I'll ring – let's be in touch!
friends say – and mean as much – but
they're already juggling balls
that toss us out of mind.

Reminders leapfrog one another
in the crazy tumble of the brain,
one stick-it note sits on the next,
musts jostle for head space.

I notice it from a year's distance.
In the slow heat of Provence
meeting meant a chance call, a stroll
through vines, a cup of real coffee.

Here, dashing between downpours,
a lengthy preamble is required.
Voicemail groans to voicemail
as we miss one another – again!

At last we speak – though don't quite
connect. Diaries are in denial.
Friday – no…Monday – not good.
What about…? Oh dear.

Breathe! A date fixed – weeks ahead
and today's impulse for friendship
grieved in a sigh of resignation
there's hardly time to feel.

The Hook

Who is barbed – you or me –
that, casting together, we snag
and tangle on one another's wants?

I jostle for position, slip,
seachange underwater, turn fish.
Your rod reels me in, soft mouth spiked,
dangling on unexpected metal.

Belly-sick, I twist away,
flop into your basket – compliant, resentful.
Blood lingers on the lips,
sours my acquiescence.

The week persists, airless with anger
until I yearn to swim and breathe again,
not to hold the hurt deep-tissue tight but

let it float away, dissolve in water,
a spurt of blood that thins
and disappears.

Recipe for Panic

I cook my own.

Here are the instructions.
Take a base of instant mix which,
when tipped, puffs and explodes
in a deep bowl of stomach.

Fold in the other ingredients:
a little urine, rich in acid,
juice of neck muscle, well squeezed,
all the segments of jellied tongue.

Spice with a few salt teardrops,
a dash of anger from the bowels,
a pinch of grated gallstones.
Taste to see if sour enough.

With a spatula scrape any lumps
still sticking in the throat.
Throw the mixture in a Mind brand
of high-speed processor.

Set the blades rotating to slash
and churn – whip not curdle it.
When ready pour out quickly.
Pop into a pre-heated heart.

A perfect soufflé of fear will rise,
an extravaganza of anxiety
topped with a heady crust
of burnt sweet and sourness.

I make it often.

Kitchen Sink

Men pee in the sink
when nobody's looking.

Caught one once
in the weak-bladdered end of night
spraying to an old tune,
the stable splat and splash of urine,
cool white porcelain steaming.

We spoke of other things
but there his prick was,
proud and free as a stallion's,
the evening's wine tracing
a faultless arc of gold.

I'd pee in the sink too –
if I could reach it.

Fighting the Morning

for Greg

He likes to argue with the radio. Its voices wake us
as the dawn slits in. We grunt into our tea,
slow to uncurl from the familiar sweat of night
but roll apart when flinty politicians start to clash.

A few light flare-ups launch his morning exercise.
He bellows questions, pokes at answers, stokes
a conflagration of MPs, whiz-kids, money-men,
urges me to join him in fanning flames.

Hidden in the quilt's warm hollows I cower,
feather-muffled from disaster, blind at this hour
to the nation's fate. World stuff may rouse him – I
want only to savour one small cup of calm

before another battle claims me – gridlock day
with stalled children to be coaxed or hand-pushed,
heavy from their beds. Let others feed or douse the fires
– I need my strength for getting up.

VI

The Artist's Line

*(inspired by Paul Klee's painting, **City in
the Intermediate Realm**, painted after his
visit to Tunisia in 1914)*

He takes his line for a walk,
surprised how it grows and grows.
He offers it pen or paint or chalk,
leaves it free to follow its nose.

It runs ahead, sets a cracking pace
larking with squirls and squiggles.
Against that glowing sky-gold space
it hops and twirls and giggles.

With circles, squares and curling hoop
it shapes a geometric city,
zigs and zags and loops the loop –
in hot Saharan sand turns witty.

Into church and minaret it roams
where midday cross and crescent sleep,
draws round all the different domes,
uniting them in one long sweep.

But when he thinks to call it back
it disobeys, laughs, splits in two,
each shoots off on a separate tack.

He waits

Cut-outs in Blue

(a tribute to Matisse who in his eighties worked
with cut-outs rather than painting directly on canvas)

(1)

Matisse at Eighty

Bed-bound or wheel-chaired, the artist
works his delicate scissors. Spirit flames
and sparks as he snips the painted pieces,
curves and angles, sticks, moves, moves again,
plays with setting fluid blue on white.

His girl is cut from sea and sky.
Tropical midday blue flows unclouded
in the arching wave of breasts, curled thighs,
soft roll of neck and sweeping spine –
fruits rounded by exotic light.

Like a glass-cutter he probes the heart of
flux and form, carves deep into the quick
of colour, chasing the sapphire's hidden flash.

(2)

Studies for the Blue Nude

What is she doing, the blue lady?
Nymph, mermaid, yogi, dancer,
she is flowing thigh, curled leg,
spheres of breast and rounded neck,
trail of soft arm circling a caress.

Another elbow juts in sharper angle
as, jig-sawed, bits of bliss fall into place.
The channel of her blue vagina
is cut and penetrated by liquid white,
holy conjunction of flow and form.

(3)

The Creation Dance

Is this Eve sitting bent-kneed, showered by apples?
Adam senses the female curves mirrored
behind him: open legs, rounded breasts, circling spine,

the feminine flow of form, liquid in primary blue.
She reaches back, leaning into the snake-tongued,
monkey-man thrust of the first creation dance.

They are alpha and omega, penetration and surrender,
sea and sky. The curve of falling apples is playful,
tempting, a reminder of what has come between them.

Picasso's Women

A Series

*(in response to the film, **Surviving Picasso**, and to Picasso's art – particularly the works named)*

At Work

He slices, dices, cubes his woman,
reconstructs her in fog-blue hues,
breaks pain-bright colour
into mad conjunctions,
hacks off pieces of himself,
saws them into female shapes
reducing form to fragments.

He elevates her curve and flow,
madonna whispered in pencil
soft-washed with liquid light until,
in restless rage, he topples and
dissects her into whore or slave,
or like a matador woos, teases, pricks,
thrusts with one sharp deceit.

In art as in life he begets himself.
Through decades of unbearable age,
sixties, seventies, eighties,
his seed spills or grows fertile
on the threshold of innovation.
A new model unclothes a new phase
before she dies, guillotined, immortal

War

*(from **Guernica**, 1937)*
On the high scaffold he struts, commands
an empty canvas, sets his women to
scratch, spit, tussle for him –
he both cock and prize of the fight.

56

Satisfied at the blood they draw, he paints.
White light jags from a naked bulb, sears
mouths filled with teeth and screams.
Heads roll in the gutter, breasts are lopped
into piles, blood runs black in the street.

A horse flames. A bull stands sliced in half –
it at least is used to dying. Women kneel,
hear their own thrown-back heads
crunch and howl in the smoke.

At home his women battle on.
He takes out his heart, stamps on it.

Age

*(from **Portrait of Francoise** (1946)*
Her youth sits cross-legged at his feet and waits.
Owl-sharp eyes pin her to the canvas, bore into her sap
as his pencil swirls in her flow. She is playfellow,
madonna, mistress, mother. She is the tree of life.

The arm she leans on is the trunk that roots and channels
her strong beauty. Her wild curls play like willow, toss
round petal eyes, curving cheek, and full-moon face that
mirror the womb in which she carries new life.

He, bald as a bullet, with white shorts and bare torso,
tips the wink to the world with his nursery motifs.
Childish, he may climb her tree but cannot bear its fruit,
he may scatter seeds but not regain the sapling years.

His lines flow through her, shade into a deeper mystery
he cannot penetrate. Though he captures her
he will never own her. Though he replaces her
he will grow older still – he will

They're Biting

(exploring Paul Klee's seascape of the same name)

A plump sun floats in its own reflection
on the green-watered, sand-gold sludge
and gloats. Though it swims in the heart
of the puzzle, we know it won't sink.
                    !
Other shapes float in the space –
a ship's bell, sense of sails, the ship of death.
Tail bones fan the horizon like cheeky flags
waving for attention, and in the foreground
one sea-smart tiddler dives deeper.
                    !
The transparent water glows, shows
a tangle of lines that cross, uncross
in a weedy maze finding their own route
to fish whose dazed eyes widen
waiting for the punch-line.
                    !
Klee plays, reeling in the future,
zooms with x-ray vision
on the fat, fleshy fish and his out-size pal,
a mean-mouthed thug who swims at his side,
exposes them skinned, gutted, filleted,
reduced to skeletal bone.
                    !
They see it coming, the last gasp,
loss of water, the glare above the waves,
read their fate in the bait –
but take it anyway – an elemental error.
                    !
The fisher stick man with his ink-blot son
thinks he's the one in charge,
the getter not the got. Underwater
sands shift and cloud their emerald bed.
A dark exclamation mark grins.
                    !

VII

Fucking Finished!

Don't give a fuck!
he sneers. *Past it!*
Grey fingers mumble,
can't hook clear
the red glob
snagged
in scrag end of throat.

Guts, lungs gasp,
giving out.
Don't give a fuck for that –
nor for the sharp-pincered crab
eating his throat.

Sucks!
Won't swear there
much longer.
Fuck it!

*

Throat clamped.
Can't swear now,
can't speak,
no pump-punctured breath
coming through,
heart stuck too,
gives up.

Smiles at his rotten luck –
what the

With Clean Shoes

Wash before prayers. Check clothes, knives,
razors, box-cutters. Make sure you are clean
and your clothes, including shoes, are clean.

Prepared for mass murder by ritual devotion,
he speeds through the pain barrier
believing he can enter Paradise soaked

in a cocktail of blood and vodka, soiled
by bladders that open pending impact – but no,
never with the blasphemy of dirty feet.

At zero hour a fireball bursts, the sky
is smoke, rubble, fumes, bodies and body bits
thrown into air that will never freshen again.

Only two open-winged birds, spun clear
like blackened doves, hold their form in dying.
Skyscrapers, murderers and murdered mix

and roll in a concentration that blocks the light.
Those below are coated in the thick white ash
of other people's lives. They breathe human dust.

Note: Mohammed Atta is believed to have
led the attack on the Twin Towers on 9/11.

Mrs Gallagher

Aluminium-cool,
the zimmer's bars contain
her hurry in a shuffle.
Eyes that swim to meet us

plead bail, her soft-lit face
shadowed with longing
to escape this Robben Island
for those whose crime is age.

It's cold here, isn't it?
Repeatedly she tests
the waters, shrinks back
marooned on vinyl rock.

A meanness of heating,
nylon cardy, lack of hugs
all chill below the norm
of Irish village life. This,

in part, she understands.
They've no fire, you see!
Her thinned voice searches
for its old round brogue.

Herself she'd always offer
an open peat-fire welcome,
spacious chat, a smile,
a sugared cup of tea.

She's nothing now to give
except her smuggled tears.
We take them up and cry,
believing still we'll get away.

By the Pool

for Scal

Your space fills the chair.
The wasps would have bothered you.
Death thins them away.

VIII

Back to Now

A Zen Meditation

Face
the wall,
draw shadows
on its whiteness.
(How is *he* getting on? He seems so still.)
Thoughts flock like pigeons wheeling on ploughed fields,
light on paint bumps,
open windows,
bird-talk,
bells.

Hands
flutter,
shoulders squirm
and curl, eyes itch,
mind chatters to the dangerous silence,
longing for collapse, for coffee, anything
but just being
in the still,
the here
now.

Face
again
tomorrow
how winter hard
it is to wait on stripped and hedgeless fields,
leave seeded clods unturned, sharp blades at rest
and let them lie
accepting
what is
is.